Advanced Catfishing Made Easy

Brad Durick

Author- Brad Durick
Editor- Jill Hobbs
Graphics- Ann White

ISBN-13: 978-0692621837
ISBN-10: 0692621830

DEDICATION

This book is dedicated to every catfish angler of every level who loves to tangle with our whiskered friends.

Remember- "It's About the Fight!"

CONTENTS

FOREWORD

Catfishing has changed since I first started fishing for them on the Little Rock River, a small stream in Northwest Iowa near where I grew up in the 1950s and early 1960s. Those were great times to be a kid in love with the outdoors. We biked everywhere, with .22 rifles in tow to plink cans at the town dump. In fall, nearby farms had squirrels, rabbits and pheasants to hunt. During summer, when we weren't playing baseball, we explored the river. No Trespassing signs were nonexistent. And parents didn't worry if you spent most of a day without checking in.

Yet all was not perfect. We had boundless enthusiasm for trying to catch channel catfish, but we weren't good at it. We had Johnson spincast reels, glass rods, monofilament line, and fished with cut minnows or worms on Aberdeen hooks. So it wasn't tackle so much as not knowing where fish were and what they were doing—and how to use that tackle appropriately.

It was all a mystery we seemingly had no way to master. There was nowhere to go to learn how to proceed, even though Jason Lucas was at the time writing masterfully about largemouth bass in the pages *Sports Afield*. And Joe Brooks was writing passionately about trout in *Outdoor Life*. There was no champion for catfish and catfishing.

So, I discovered one of my life missions. I had the opportunity to learn about catfishing and to write about it for others to enjoy in the pages of *In-Fisherman* magazine, starting in the mid 1980s. Some of the best of that writing is found in *Life & Times In Catfish Country—All Along The Road To The Modern Age of Catfishing*. It compliments the more recent books by Capt. Brad Durick, an exceptional angler and guide who is at his best analyzing field data and turning it into information anglers can draw from to catch more fish.

These days, with catfishing on a roll, so to speak, with the number of catfish anglers holding strong at about 7 million participants year after year, we continue to fine tune fundamentals and dabble in topics heretofore unexplored. Durick's first book, *Cracking the Channel Catfish Code*, is a solid step forward in further understanding the ways of our finny friend.

Here, in *Advanced Catfishing Made Easy*, he offers a vest-pocket guide to solving problems you face in the field, with a system that makes perfect sense and is easy to put into play, no matter where you fish in North America. It's like having an expert in the field with you, your mentor and friend, helping to ensure that you fish with confidence and success.

Good fishing to you. Harvest catfish selectively and have fun.

Doug Stange, Editor In Chief, In-Fisherman

ADVANCED CATFISHING MADE EASY

Congratulations on taking the next step to successful catfishing! Catfish are an amazing and popular fish whose popularity is growing by leaps and bounds. At the same time, there is not much new information about catfish and how to catch them out there. We all know the basics but not much about changing gears and adjusting our tactics on the fly with ever-changing conditions.

This guide is designed to take fishing with you to aid you in making adjustments; in the end, helping you catch more fish. There are a few assumptions that are going to be made. First, we are going to assume that you have had fairly recent access to a weather report or have a smart phone with you on the trip to keep up to date on changing conditions. This will help should you need to see what is going to arise.

Once you fine-tune the methods here to match your way of fishing and your body of water, you **WILL** be a better catfish angler.

In time, these steps will be automatic and you should not need this book any longer. Then it will become a reference guide for when the times get tough on the water.

This book will be more specific to channel catfish but many of these tactics will also work for the other species of catfish. If this book is a success, there will be follow up guides that will cater specifically for other catfish.

LET'S GET STARTED

We are going to assume you know the basic seasons in the life of a catfish. Spring cold water, pre spawn, spawn, post spawn/summer, late summer/fall, fall, fall cold water and ice. As we move forward, we will break the sections of this guide into these basic seasons. Then we will add in the variables that you may be facing and offer some solutions to tackle those variables.

Simply find the season that you are currently fishing. Collect some current data on the conditions, turn to the proper page and make your adjustments. Call this a "pick your own catfish adventure" guide.

Keep in mind that we are dealing with nature and its creatures. Sometimes no matter what we do the fish don't wish to cooperate. With that, the systems used in this guide are proven techniques of success. No matter the season, you will stay more consistent in your catch rates.

If you do not know the seasons of a catfish or are just getting started, we recommend that you read *Catfish Fever* (1989) by the In-Fisherman staff.

To further understand the catfish and dig deeper into water, weather and patterns and how catfish work, we recommend *Cracking the Channel Catfish Code* (2013) by Brad Durick.

TOOLS YOU WILL NEED

Smart phone and/or computer with internet connection
Thermometer
Rods
Reels
Line
Sinkers
Hooks
Other fine fishing equipment
Confidence

Ok, you knew the last part, but you will need to do a little research on your own to make this system work to your advantage. The easiest way is to simply look up a few things on your smart phone or computer.

You will need to find out some current conditions of the body of water you want to fish and the current weather or weather trends (usually three to five days of weather data).

Www.wunderground.com for historical weather to put together trends from the past few days.

Www.USGS.org for water data in your area. This will provide gauge height, flow and sometimes temperature on most bodies of water.

Most USGS gauges do not have water temperature included, so you will have to use the reading on your electronics or do it the old fashioned way and carry a thermometer with you. There are special sinking thermometers on the market for fishing that are small and easy to use on the spot.

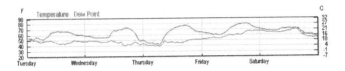

The above graph illustrates a warming trend. With this simple graph (www.wunderground.com) you can determine warming water conditions before you ever get to the river or lake.

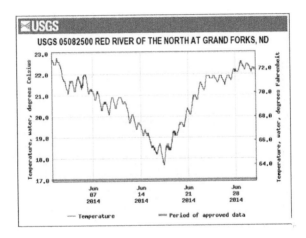

The graph above shows trends in water temperature for a month. With these USGS graphs you can quickly determine rising or falling water trends. Unfortunately, most USGS gauges do not provide this information. If your local gauge does not provide temperature you will have to use the weather trends graph mentioned previously.

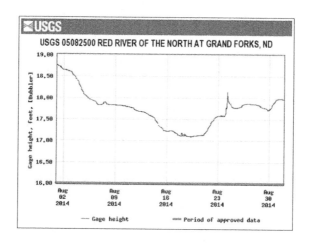

The graph above demonstrates river gauge height for a month. With these USGS graphs, you can quickly determine a rising or falling water trend.

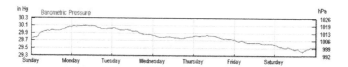

This graph from www.wunderground.com shows a trend in barometric pressure over a week. What is says is that the week was cloudy to partly cloudy and led up to a huge storm on the weekend. This is just another illustration of how watching trends can help you predict catfish patterns and how they will react. This graph says heavy feeding up until the storm on Saturday. (We did document this trend with great fishing all week.)

INTERPRETING WEATHER DATA

We already mentioned www.wunderground.com for looking up weather trends. There is a lot of mention of barometric trends in this book.

The easiest way to get these trends is to log onto the above site, type in your zip code to receive a current forecast. With this forecast you can now see an hourly outlook for the day including a barometer prediction. This will give you an idea of what is about to happen. It will also give you history data allowing you to look at the last few days or week of conditions.

This will show you the trends in barometer, sunshine and temperature. This matched with the forecast for the day you can usually figure out what the water temperatures are to establish how you are going to attack a day on the water.

Another thing to keep in mind is that weather norms and trends can change in a heartbeat. For the purpose of this guide we use normal weather trends. Keep in mind that things happen (such as the Christmas storms and flooding of 2015) and we have to adjust accordingly to stay safe and successful.

BAROMETER

There are many theories to the barometer and why fish and animals react to it the way they do. In this book we take a totally different approach to how fish react to barometer.

One theory is that as the barometer changes from high to low pressure and vice versa the fish's air bladder takes time for gas to escape or equalize so the fish feels right in the water column. It says that as a fish moves around to find a comfort zone, this is where they will be easier to catch. It is also says that after a large front passes the fish simply does not feel good and quits eating until things level out after a few hours or a few days.

A second theory is that air pressure on water is so minute that fish would never even notice it. Instead the barometer is a determination of the sun and the catfish react to the intensity or lack of sun.

The theory we use in this book is that the other two may play a small part in how barometer works with fish, but it also introduces another theory that is so simple it is almost hard to believe.

Fish and animals do not have weather forecasters to tell them what conditions are on the way. Instead, they have to use their internal instincts to help them survive.

With this, fish and animals can sense a negative weather event off in a distance. They have no way of knowing how bad it might be, so they feed in preparation for the negative. This explains the feeding frenzy leading up to a storm and the lack of feeding after a big storm.

Based on the metabolic needs of a catfish, it makes sense that a catfish feeds in preparation to the negative, lays out of the way during the storm and is simply full after the storm.

OBSERVATION: Deer and catfish are very similar when it comes to barometer. If you see a lot of deer feeding during the day you can usually fish for catfish aggressively as this is an indicator of a falling barometer.

TIME OF DAY

Everything in this book is going to be based on fishing in the daytime, with the occasional mention of other times. Catfish are long thought to be a nighttime only fish. In reality, they move into and out of feeding areas (usually during the night). During certain times of the season, time of day does not matter. Other times, time of day does matter as to where and how you fish. We will take this into consideration.

If you are a boat angler, you have the ability to go to the fish during different times of day. If you are limited to the shore, you have to consider this more and let the fish come to you if you can't go to them.

Daytime- Page 18
Low light- Page 18
Nighttime- Page 19

Daytime

Daytime catfishing once had a bad reputation, with many saying that catfish just simply do not bite during the day. This is mostly due to the fact that decades ago most catfishing was done from shore.

While many catfish anglers are still shore-bound, many more have taken to fishing from a boat and a whole new world has opened up to them.

Catfish do slow down feeding sometimes during daylight and high sun situations. This is a case when anglers in boats have the advantage because they can move to deeper holes or position themselves into heavier structure where fish are holed up during the day.

During the spring, pre spawn and fall, when the water tends to be cooler daytime catfishing is known to be better because the sun is actively heating the water up, thus getting the catfish to feed.

Low Light

By low light times, we are referring to morning sunrise and evening sunset. When the sun is low catfish can be caught in transition, moving to and from their feeding areas to where they hole up during the day.

To many catfish anglers, these times of day can be the best time of day. During these times, flats and edges of holes between and current seams set up to be great night feeding areas.

These times of day is usually very good fishing no matter what part of the season the catfish are in.

Nighttime

In most catfish circles, "nighttime is the right time" to tangle with old Mr. Whiskers. As mentioned earlier this is because catfish tend to feed at night and move shallow to chase the minnows, frogs and other creepy crawlies they want to eat.

During the night, catfish move to the front of holes and out onto the flats between holes into faster water. They also move to the shallow water along the banks in search of food.

This is the time the shore anglers can really make hay. They can fish the easier-to-reach current seams or the cutouts along the bank.

Boat anglers can position themselves right along the same lines and have the ability to adjust the bait placement along these lines and in these little feeding "nooks".

BAIT

Bait selection varies in different parts of the country. For that reason, this book will not address the topic of bait selection. Based on your geographic area you will need to research baits and experiment and implement your own bait regimen.

The easiest way is to find a local bait shop to ask about what local baits are the best for your style of catfishing. Another great way to find regional information on bait selection is through a local or area internet talk forum.

MOVING

Move-move-move

The concepts and patterns in this book are solid, but not every spot is created equal. If you are trying a pattern and it simply is not working, try moving to a different spot before you abandon the pattern.

Spots may not work within a pattern for a variety of reasons. It could be that one factor or another was not right or as simple as someone fished the same spot before you arrived.

HIGH WATER

Rivers rise; high water and flooding situations happen at some point or another. During these high water periods, safety should be the number one concern of all anglers. Staying calm is the key to dealing with the increased flows and the debris and other floating matter that can come with it.

Catfish usually respond positively to high water. During high water the catfish move to the outer edges of the river that are referred to in this book as "secondary channels" or "secondary seams". Knowing this information, you can use these same systems to keep fishing. Once you get a feel for it you, will see good success.

During high water, the ticket is to look for these secondary channels in areas right along the cut banks of the river, the back of inside corners or even out of the river altogether in the flood plain.

It is also a wonderful time to start fishing tributaries or creeks that connect to the main river. Catfish will move up these tributaries and channels to escape the heavy currents that are in the river. Once in the smaller rivers or creeks, simply fish the same systems.

Remember, please be safe.

OBSERVATION: Sometimes during a flood situation when you get into tributaries and creeks, the current will run the wrong direction because of the pressure from the main river. The best fishing is away from this and where the current in the tributary is running the proper direction.

ELIMINATE PATTERNS

Sometimes it is easier to eliminate patterns rather than find them. How this works is you hit a pattern that you don't think is the answer. If you don't catch fish in the first two or three spots, you just discovered what doesn't work and eliminated 50% of your fishable spots.

An example of this is you had been on a good bite just off the secondary current seams but you know the fish could be moving to mid-river holes. You have not fished in a few days and want to make the most of your time on the water. You start the day in a few tried and true mid-river holes. If you don't catch anything in two spots, then switch back to the secondary current seams and boom!

By doing this to eliminate patterns, you waste less time on what worked a few days ago and may not work today.

This is a technique used by many professional tournament anglers during prefishing to establish a pattern.

SPOT ROTATION

Spot rotation is a topic that may or may not pertain to your fishing. If you fish more than a couple days per week, this does make a difference.

After you fish a spot two times in a row you may see the catch rates fall off more and more with each consecutive day.

For that reason, if you are fishing consecutive days it might be advisable to leave spots alone for two to three days between visits. Doing this will help good spots and fishing areas recover and be more productive in the long run.

This goes for community holes that are no secret. Be a bit selective when you fish these spots to avoid being the last one into the spots and wasting your time fishing water that has been fished out.

KEEPING A JOURNAL

Keeping a journal of days on the water is something that everyone says is a great idea, yet very few people actually do.

Many people who start keeping journals of their days on the water write down everything about every fish and that is not necessary.

The system in this book follows trends and patterns. Weather and water trends are recorded online so there is no need to keep all that information in your journal until you compile the data for later use and then you can look it up.

For patterning purposes, keep track of what patterns were working, what didn't work, what changed, how many fish were caught and if there was anything that stood out from the outing.

When you look back on it, you will remember the day. If something isn't going well on a future trip, you can look back at the similar conditions and fine-tune the pattern.

Remember, for this catfish system we are using current trending data to establish patterns, not memories of the past on a calendar. The journal is a tool to fill in the blanks to solidify your patterns in the future.

CONFIDENCE

Confidence is something that seems to be missing in fishing sometimes and without it you will never be what you can be no matter what you do.

Fishing takes confidence. Of course, to get confidence you will have to experience some failures along the way. It is just part of learning. Remember the saying from when you were little, "If at first you don't succeed, try, try again"?

This book is here to help you sidestep some of the failures and gain more confidence in your catfishing. It will help you think your way through the tough times and get a game plan for your outing. You will then see more success and also gain more confidence.

World famous bass angler Kevin Van Dam says, "If you don't think you are going to win, why even show up?"

This is where knowledge and confidence come together and we want you to have that confidence every time you hit the water.

MAN MADE ISSUES

Most of the research for these tactics was conducted on a natural river with only a few man made dams. In many areas of the country, agriculture and industry have changed the river systems through dams and channelization.

While a river is a river and a fish is a fish, this does change things in how the fish react during certain conditions. It makes man made structure more important and it also makes reading a river crucial when venturing out.

Agriculture has created drains and canals to let water off fields faster to protect the crops. This also means that rivers and reservoirs now rise and fall faster than in more natural riparian times of the rivers.

CATFISH SEASONS

	JAN	FEB	MAR	APR	MAY	JUN	JUL	AUG	SEP	OCT	NOV	DEC
North	1	1	1,2	2	2,3	3,4	4,5	5	5,6,7	7	7,8	1
Middle	1,2	2	2,3	3	3,4	3,4,5	5	5	5,6	6,7	7,8	8,1
South	2	2	2,3	3	3,4	4,5	5	5	5	5,6	6,7	7,8

1- Ice
2- Spring Cold Water
3- Pre Spawn
4- Spawn

5- Post Spawn/Summer
6- Late Summer/Fall
7- Fall
8- Fall Cold Water

Adapted from Catfish Fever- In Fisherman 1989

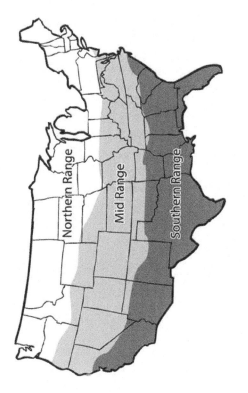

Northern Range
Mid Range
Southern Range

This map was adapted with permission from In-Fisherman's Catfish Fever (1989)

SPRING COLD WATER

Spring Cold Water (32-50 degrees)

The cold water period is the time in the early spring
(winter in some areas) when the catfish are slow and their
metabolism is low but starting to come alive. During the
cooler part of this period, the catfish will tend to stay put
in the deeper holes unless there is heavy spring current
coming at them, in which case they will move. As the
water temperature gets closer to 50 degrees, the fish will
start to move shallow and feed on dead fish and other
food that is turning up from winter.

Water temperature 32-40 degrees- Page 31
Water temperature 40-50 degrees- Page 32
Is the water level rising?- Page 33
Is the water level stable to falling?- Page 34
Is the barometer rising?- Page 35
Is the barometer falling?- Page 36
Light Conditions?- Page 37
Water Clarity?- Page 38

Spring Cold Water
Water Temperature 32-40 Degrees

This is the time when catfish are waking up from winter. The catfish are starting to feed, looking for dead food or more rotten baits that are left over from winter.

In southern climates this is just a cold water period, but in northern climates, you may be just breaking loose of ice cover.

At the beginning of this period the catfish may be holding in or near the wintering holes, but as things warm up to near 40 degrees, the fish will begin to seek out warmer water. This is a time to look at very shallow, wind-blown shores of lakes or out of the current on rivers.

If you are in a spring high water period, the catfish will move off the wintering holes and into tributaries or right along the bank out of the current. Look at slack water and/or tributaries that they may have moved into to avoid the higher flows.

On lakes or in rivers with no spring rise, start at the wintering holes working the break lines and edges of the hole for active catfish.

Consider old frozen baits, sour cut bait or dead fish that has washed up along the bank.

Bites will probably be very light. Downsizing weight and gear may be in order to detect bites.

Spring Cold Water
Water Temperature 40-50 Degrees

Things are heating up and the catfish are still a bit sluggish but starting to get a little more active. This is the time that their metabolism begins to come alive. The fish will start to hunt. They tend to look for warmer water during this time.

As the water warms up, river catfish will start to move to the current seams to begin the pre spawn feed.

Start looking at faster water and current breaks. If they are acting a bit sluggish or not feeding on the breaks, look at structure such as snags or rocks to fish near.

It is a day-by-day bite depending on how the water is warming or cooling during this period. Look at north shores (facing south) for active fish, since that bank gets the brunt of the sun during the heat of the day. Also think shallow during this time.

OBSERVATION: This is a time when bushes and trees begin to bud. When you see this you will know that the pre spawn is just around the corner.

Spring Cold Water
Water Level Rising

This is the time a spring flood may hit due to runoff or because spring rains have set in. If this is happening, start looking out of the current along the banks. Don't be afraid to look very shallow, maybe 1-3 feet of water.

When some rivers go out of the banks during spring floods, catfish can be caught very shallow in agricultural fields.

Catfish will also run up ditches or tributaries to escape the heavy current. These small streams and tributaries can be goldmines during these times.

Many lakes don't have to worry about the spring flood and high water times. Should a lake rise very fast during this time, the same applies. Find the streams and creeks that run into the lakes and follow the catfish.

OBSERVATION: Notice where beavers are building their houses. Beavers are the kings of avoiding damaging currents. If you know where the beaver houses are, you know where the secondary current seams are. Beaver houses can also make good structure to hold catfish during high water.

Spring Cold Water
Water Level Stable to Falling

If the water level is stable to falling, you will want to look in the current seams and near structure. This should be a water condition that will bring spring catfish to life.

With temperatures below 40 degrees, the catfish should still be in or near the wintering holes. A light sensitive rod with a jig can be a deadly combination in this situation, as the catfish are still sluggish and won't put up the big runs. As they warm up some, you will have to upgrade to heavier gear more suited for catfish.

When the water warms into the upper 40s and 50s, you will have to use regular catfish gear. The fish will begin to move to the shallows and hunt. They will also begin to work the current seams and hang out near structure.

In lakes, the fish will move out of the wintering holes to the shallows or the windblown shores to begin hunting and getting ready for the upcoming spawn.

Spring Cold Water
Barometer Rising

This is the one time of the year when a rising barometer is
to our advantage. A rising barometer tends to mean sunny
conditions, sun means rising water temperatures and
warming temperatures mean increasing metabolism.

Until the water temperatures reach the high 40s, the rising
barometer and sun are a blessing to catfish and kick the
season into high gear.

Spring Cold Water
Barometer Falling

A falling barometer can be a good thing during this period because catfish instinct kicks in to prepare for the negatives, which may spur a feeding frenzy.

With the lower metabolisms of the season, it doesn't take much food to sustain catfish. Once the front pushes through, the catfish can get very sluggish right after the barometer begins its swing back up. This may last a couple days.

Before the front actually moves in, start to fish a bit more aggressively to find the catfish that are feeding before the front.

After the front moves through, sit on the spots longer and fish smaller baits to try to draw the active fish out to feed.

Spring Cold Water
Light Conditions

Light conditions fall into the same category as a rising to high barometer. When the water is cold, the catfish want the heat. This means that clear skies and high sun can work to your advantage because the water is warming.

As the temperature moves into the mid to high 40s, the fish are more active and the light conditions will become increasingly important as to how it will impact the bite.

Spring Cold Water Period
Water Clarity

Water clarity during this time ranges from a clear running mountain stream to the equivalent of boiling chocolate milk, depending on the type of river and the runoff situation.

In clear water, catfish will act pretty normal and maybe hang a little deeper to avoid daytime sun. You may see an increase in the bite during the low light period.

If the water is muddy with very little clarity, this can push the catfish very shallow. Generally, this is because bait fish move shallow or they are trying to get away from the debris that usually comes with very dirty water.

Don't be afraid to fish very shallow in one to three feet of water during this time.

PRE SPAWN

Pre Spawn (50-70 degrees)

The pre spawn period is typically one of the best times of year to catch catfish. They have two things on their mind and one of them is eating. It is the time of the year when they are the least susceptible to external conditions. They are bulking up from the cold water period and getting ready for the upcoming spawn. Due to the warming of the water, their metabolism is increasing exponentially (almost weekly) and they just have to eat that much more to survive, let alone prepare for the upcoming spawn.

Pre Spawn
Water Temperature 50-60 Degrees

Fifty degrees is a magic number for catfish. The metabolism of a channel catfish has increased 100 percent since 40 degrees and instinct to feed leading up to the spawn is kicking into high gear.

This is the beginning of what many call the best fishing of the year.

In rivers, start really looking at visible current along the seams to the main river channel. Look shallow, especially along south-facing shorelines that warm more quickly with the spring sun.

In lakes, also consider the south facing bank and work the wind-blown shoreline where bait comes in.

Another area of advantage in this situation is to look for dark colored bottom or gravel, as they warm more quickly than other bottoms.

This is a time to stay on the move and try different spots and patterns. Once you find the catfish, great things will happen.

Pre Spawn
Water Temperature 60-65 Degrees

Since the water temperature first reached 50 degrees, the metabolism has doubled once again and so has the daily food requirements. From 60-65 degrees, it will double yet again.

Now is the time to fish aggressively. Keep working the visible seams to the main channel; work the spots where the seams meet structure. You may want to look at mid-river holes, but they tend not to be the best areas at this time when the catfish are migrating upstream and feeding.

In lakes, the fish should be up shallow, still searching for anything they can find to eat. They will be sunning themselves on sandbars or along the south-facing banks.

Keep the bait fresh and stay on the move. Once you find active fish you most likely will find even more.

OBSERVATION: Lilacs and other bushes are blossoming at this time.

Pre Spawn
Water Temperature 65-70 Degrees

Metabolism has increased over 200% since the water temperature was 50 degrees. This is the water temperature window that is the last feeding push before the spawn begins.

This is a time when in rivers, the feeding fish tend to start moving downstream in preparation to find a nesting area. You should fish the same way as you do the rest of the pre spawn time, but keep in mind (especially if you fish near a dam or just downstream of a dam) that the catfish will move farther down.

It is critical to cover a lot of water to stay on active fish, as they are getting ready to sit on the nest.

In lakes, the fish move very shallow near weeds or rocks to set the nest.

OBSERVATION: Leaves on the trees are almost full as the pre spawn is coming to an end.

Pre Spawn
Water Temperature Rising

Stable to slow rising water temperature is the key to great fishing during the pre spawn. It has already been mentioned that metabolism is increasing exponentially and with that the instincts to prepare for spawn, hence "pre spawn".

When the water temperatures are rising during this time, the fish are on the prowl and you should fish them accordingly. Fish aggressively along the main current seams, the outside edges of structure where the current swings by and in riffle areas.

If you have a dam or structure that can be a barrier to fish travel, this is the time to work the downstream side of it. The fish are on an upstream feed and can bottle up in those locations. The best fishing can be within a mile of the dam.

As temperatures reach the 68 to 70 degree range, you will start to see more of a downstream migration in feeding begin as the fish are spreading out to find nests and move into the spawn.

Pre Spawn
Water Temperature Falling

With pre spawn being in late spring or early summer, there can be weather events that set in and will bring the water temperatures down.

If temperatures fall a small amount while in the 50s or low 60s, it can just help prolong what is many times the best bite of the year.

Should the water temperature fall off by five to ten degrees, the fish can go into a sort of shock and you will have to resort to fishing the secondary current seams. Sit on spots a little longer, tight to structure.

Waiting a couple days for the temperatures to level out and become stable is usually all it takes for the catfish to come back out and commence the pre spawn bite.

Pre Spawn
Water Level Rising

If the water levels are rising, keep working the main current seams but also start looking for structure to act as a current break.

Look for secondary current seams forming along the bank. Catfish tend to move out to the secondary seam for easier swimming, feeding and resting.

If a river is getting high (nearing flood stage), move to the secondary currents and possibly quit fishing mid river. This area will form a river by itself that will provide everything a catfish will need. Also consider feeder channels and tributaries.

This will also allow you to keep fishing safely, as debris could overtake the main river channel.

Rising water during the pre spawn is usually not a bad thing since the fish tend to feed upstream. Should the water be rising or nearing a high water event when the water temperature is about 67-72, the catfish may migrate downstream more than normal in search of an area to nest.

If water levels rise very quickly you may experience large amounts of debris. Catfish want to avoid this as much as we do. In this situation, try to find spots that are out of the current to avoid collecting grass and other debris on your lines. Usually these spots are very shallow.

Pre Spawn
Water Level Stable to Falling

If the water level is falling from a high water period or just a seasonal drop, it can go both ways. If the water is dropping very slowly, just fish as normal to the time, working the seams and structure areas. Should the water be falling six inches to a foot or more per day, get out of the current and work the off-current secondary seams, tight to structure or the bank. The back of inside corners work very well during this time.

Every river has a point where the catfish will move from the secondary to the main current. Be safe and experiment with this. You will know if they are moving out of the secondary very quickly.

Refer to drawing on page 105

Pre Spawn
Barometer Rising

A rising barometer tends to mean clear sunny skies and nice weather. During the pre spawn this does not mean a whole lot because the need to feed is so high. The sun is warming the water and actually turning the fish on due to the increase in metabolism.

Fish as you normally would without much worry about a rising barometer.

Pre Spawn
Barometer Falling

During pre spawn a slow falling barometer means more cloudy skies, but the need to feed is not going to change much unless a major drop in barometer occurs before a big storm. In this case, it may actually make the bite better as the fish prepare for the negative of the looming storm.

In the short term, keep working the faster water and current seams as the barometer drops. Once it bottoms out, if the bite slows, move off the current to the secondary current.

Also, consider working structure for sitting catfish that are holding tight and not necessarily feeding.

The same applies in lakes and ponds. Fish aggressively until right after the front passes, then slow down.

Pre Spawn
Light Conditions

Sunny

If the sun is shining, the water is warming. This is typically high or rising barometer. As the water warms, the fish will become more aggressive. Work the seams and the faster water areas. Be sure to stay on the move.

In lakes, stay on the shallows or windblown shore lines.

Cloudy

If the conditions are cloudy, there should not be much change but the catfish may move shallower due to less sun penetration in clearer water.

Chances are you will see very little change in the pre spawn bite.

Dark

If it is dark (night), the catfish just naturally move to the flats and shallower water. During pre spawn they may sometimes slow down due to the water cooling from lack of daytime heat.

In either case, fish shallow and on flats.

Pre Spawn
Water Clear

Clear water during the pre spawn will sometimes drive the catfish deeper. Occasionally, they will move to deeper water near the main current seams. In most rivers, the only time you will have to worry about this is during a very low water period.

This may also push the catfish bite to low light periods or even a night bite.

In lakes water clarity doesn't mean as much as rivers, but it can also push the catfish bite deeper to the night or under structure.

Pre Spawn
Water Cloudy or Dirty

Most rivers carry sediment (with the exception of western or mountain streams) and have less light penetration. Pre spawn tends to have spring runoff, causing the water to become even dirtier than during normal flow. This will push hunting catfish shallower than they normally go. Don't be afraid to fish in one to three feet of water if this occurs.

SPAWN

Spawn (70-74 degrees)

The spawn is the most hated time of the year by most catfish anglers. Yes, the spawn season does make life more difficult, but catfish can still be caught. First, not all fish spawn at the same time and some catfish do not spawn every year. This means that you should still be able to find pre spawn fish in feeding mode even though the spawn has begun. You should also see some post spawn fish start feeding, while the later fish are on the nest. Second, by simply understanding where catfish go to spawn and understanding a few simple tactics, you will see success.

Water temperature stable to rising?- Page 52
Water temperature falling?- Page 53
Is the water level rising?- Page 54
Is the water level stable to falling?- Page 55
Is the barometer rising?- Page 56
Is the barometer falling?- Page 57
Light Conditions?- Page 58

Spawn
Water Temperature Stable to Rising

This is what we want when the spawn kicks into full gear.
Stable water temperature over 70 degrees is key. A slow
rise in temperature is even better. This will put the females
into the nest first, then the males will move in to fan and
guard the nest.

If you hit it right when things are about to happen, you
will find the females on the nest side of a river or where
you believe the nest should be. You will also find a
number of males roaming nearby. In a river, the males will
be just along the main current seam.

After a couple days you will notice males on the nest areas
and females will be few and far between. The females are
in the resting period at this time.

Keep fishing aggressively, just like during pre spawn.
When you start catching females again (usually skinny),
you know the end has begun and to get ready for the post
spawn.

**OBSERVATION: If you have cottonwood trees in
your area they tend to drop cotton about the same
time spawn commences. This is a great indicator to
tell you when to fish for the spawn.**

Spawn
Water Temperature Falling

Should the spawn get going and a cold front roll through, the bite will quickly get tough. The active fish will have moved off the main seams and be sitting on the secondary seams or in the off current. The fish that are on the spawn beds will be even more sluggish than normal.

Sit on spots 30-40 minutes if you are sure there are fish in the area. Give them a chance to find and want the baits.

Cooling water, if it lasts long enough, can stall or extend the spawn for a few days or even weeks.

Should you notice your lines being picked up and moved from a nest area, but no sign of a hook setting, set the hook even though there is not a good strike. This is a time the males will move the bait to protect the nest and have no desire to eat the bait.

Spawn
Water Level Rising

If the spawn has set in during a period of rising water, catfish will tend to move off the main channel and into the secondary channel very shallow. They will set up shop in a hole or log jam in as little as a couple feet. Sometimes they will move upstream into tributaries to spawn.

If you have cut banks in your river not much changes, as the catfish tend to nest on the cut banks anyway.

Spawn
Water Level Stable to Falling

If the spawn is on during falling water, shallow is king, as some of the nests will be very, very shallow from being set in during higher water. Don't be afraid to cast tight to a cut bank or the shore in search of spawning fish.

Refer to drawing on page 104

Spawn
Barometer Rising

In many cases the barometer does not make much difference during the spawn. A positive to a rising or high barometer is that it tends to mean clear sunny skies, and sun warms the water more which helps incubate the eggs faster. This is a time when it is even better to fish south-facing shorelines where the water will warm more quickly.

One time that there is a negative to a rising barometer during the spawn is when it indicates a storm has recently passed and the catfish have not recovered yet. This normally lasts two or three days.

During the spawn, there really isn't much to change in pattern and presentation after a front moves through.

Spawn
Barometer Falling

If the barometer is falling, it means there is some sort of negative weather on the way. While spawning, fish are not interested in feeding, so you may not see much action either way.

Catfish that are not on the nest or coming out of the nest will be affected. With a looming storm or front, these fish may feed aggressively in preparation.

As soon as the front passes, get back off current or into deeper, more stagnant water where the catfish will recover just like during any other time of the year.

Spawn
Light Conditions

Spawning catfish tend to like sunlight. The bright sun warms the water increasing their metabolism. The water temperatures are already over 70 degrees, the sun helps mature the eggs and moves the season along by getting all of the fish on and off the nest.

Extended cloudy conditions cool the water and slow the progression of the spawn.

POST SPAWN/SUMMER

Post Spawn/Summer

For the reason that many anglers don't even notice the transition from post spawn to summer pattern, we will discuss the two together for purpose of simple patterning.

Post spawn and summer are the times of year when it tends to be the hottest. Some call it the "dog days of summer". Most old school catfish anglers shift to a night bite during this time and that is certainly not wrong.

Catfish do bite during the day, but they are spread out and weather plays into the bite more than any other time of the season, with the exception of spawn.

Water temperature rising- Page 60
Water temperature falling- Page 61
Water temperature over 85 degrees- Page 62
Is the water level rising? Page 63
Is the water level stable to falling? Page 64
Is the barometer rising? Page 65
Is the barometer falling? Page 66
Light Conditions? Page 67

Post Spawn/Summer
Water Temperature 70+ Degrees and Rising

After the spawn, water temperatures are typically rising or stabilizing as summer sets. This is the time when the combination of increased metabolism, matched with the need to feed after a long spawn, puts the catfish into high gear. A catfish needs approximately six percent of its body weight daily just to survive and even more to recover and grow. This means that the need to feed is high and the action should be good.

Catfish during this time will be fairly spread out and take up residence in a general area of a river or lake. They will eat and rest in that same general area. Lateral movement comes into play during this time of year.

Deeper water in holes or near structure with current are the hunting and ambush areas catfish use during this time of year. Start fishing at the heads of holes, edges of snags or outside edges of the river near faster water.

In lakes, they move to the deeper water on expansive flats, old river channels or other structure or break lines.

Refer to drawing on pages 106, 107, 110

Post Spawn/Summer
Water Temperature 70+ Degrees and Falling

In most cases during the summer, this is a situation when a large storm or cold front takes place. It could be a few days of sustained cool temperatures or large amounts of rain running in, cooling the water temperature.

This does not affect lakes nearly as much as it affects rivers.

When this happens, the fish will move laterally out of the main currents to the secondary seam, deeper into the snags or to the middle and back of holes. They will "sulk" so to speak and be negative.

Depending on the severity of the cool down, the catfish will start feeding again in three to four days.

Refer to drawing on pages 105, 108

Post Spawn/Summer
Water Temperature Over 85 Degrees

In the "dog days of summer" water temperatures can get into the 80s and even the 90s. When water temperatures creep over 85 degrees and into the 90s, the fish begin to change again. This time other factors can come into play. The fish may overheat or the oxygen level in the water can see more depletion than during other times of year. You may see the fishing action slow down and the fish begin to be sluggish due to this lack of oxygen.

If this happens, look for current in a river or running water of any kind. These areas provide better oxygen in the water to promote more feeding.

Also look for deeper water that may be cooler. Usually these holes are mid-range holes that provide some cooler water.

The very deepest holes tend not to hold catfish in rivers during this time, as the oxygenated water flows over the top of a deeper hole.

This is the perfect time for night fishing.

Post Spawn/Summer
Water Level Rising

Normally this time of the year has fairly stable water levels, but some years rain comes and that changes things.

A small rise in water levels or a heavy rain event can turn the bite on, especially if the water temperature is in the high 70s or 80s. This fresh oxygenated water can really kick the bite into high gear. Fish the mid-river holes and current seams and outside edges of snags.

Sometimes you will see fish move up to dams or creek mouths after storms on a feeding frenzy.

In lakes, you may not see the water level jump like rivers, but should a big rain hit, look to the edges of holes or creek mouths where fresh water is running in.

Should the rains be too much and rivers start to get high or near flood stage, look to the secondary currents just like you would during pre spawn.

Refer to drawing on page 105

Post Spawn/Summer
Water Level Stable to Falling

Falling water is the norm during this time of year in most places. The spring rains have long passed and now it is just the occasional thunderstorm bringing in water. The heat of summer evaporation in full swing. All of this is a contributing factor to the warmer water.

With this considered normal, it is time to fish the most aggressive currents you can find. You will also want to check smaller mid-river holes. Don't stay in any one hole too long, as the fish are usually spread out.

With the exception of a huge storm that recently pushed through or a larger drop in water temperature, you can usually fish this pattern quickly, working spots for 15-20 minutes.

This can be a great time to drift flats on lakes.

Post Spawn/Summer
Barometer Rising

When the barometer is rising, as previously mentioned, the sun is usually high, which makes the water hotter. This is not a good thing, as the fish are already sluggish and the pounding heat will force them to sit tighter during the day.

Fishing low light times of the day or nighttime can be your best bet to avoid the hot direct sun.

Fish faster visible current seams or holes with current.

Even a single cloud blocking the sun can spur a bite during this time.

This is a great time for drifting or night fishing.

Post Spawn/Summer
Barometer Falling

A falling barometer when the water is this hot can be a godsend for both the fish and your comfort. It will usually bring a southerly wind, which can cause waves and break up the direct sun.

When the barometer is falling or a front is moving in, as mentioned earlier, the sky tends to be cloudy which again will take the direct sunlight off the water and may make the fish more active.

Should a front be setting up to produce a large storm, the fish will try to come out to feed and prepare for the unknown. The bite should get better as the storm gets closer.

OBSERVATION: Generally after the drop in barometer and the storm front, the winds will turn to the west or north indicating that the front has pushed through.

Post Spawn/Summer
Light Conditions

Sunny

If the sun is shining and it is hot out, sometimes the catfish will move to holes and sit tight until bait drops right in front of them. A little wind to cause a ripple on the water or even a single cloud covering the sun for a few moments can be enough to spur a bite.

Cloudy

Cloudy days (typically lower barometer) during this period will get the fish moving a little more and the bite will pick up. Lower light in warm water usually puts catfish in the mood to feed.

Dark

It is nighttime and the catfish during this period will come out and hunt. Fish the edges of the main current seams, shallow flat, areas along shore and shallow, faster water areas. It is nothing for a catfish to move one-quarter to one-half mile to find a meal during this time. Being ready is the key.

LATE SUMMER/EARLY FALL

Late Summer/Early Fall

When the late summer cool down begins and the water temperatures drop from the 70s to 60s and possibly into the high 50s, this pattern fits in with each incremental drop in temperature. The catfish's seasonal instincts kick in telling them to feed up for the long winter ahead. The fish will slow down for a couple days but pick right back up to feeding when the water temperature drops, slows, stabilizes or shows a slight increase.

One thing to consider during this time is catfish will follow bait fish to what are considered abnormal areas, such as very shallow in very hot water during the day. This is due to instincts kicking in telling the fish it is time to feed in preparation for fall and winter when the metabolisms will be very low.

Late Summer/Early Fall
Water Temperature Rising

This is a very tricky situation because if the water is still warm due to a late summer, the rising water temperature really doesn't increase the bite much during this time.

In a normal year, you will see a slow drop in the temperature as the days become shorter and the nights cooler. This is when a rise in water temperature can really turn catfish on.

When the water temperature is in the 50-60 degree range and on a slow decline, a couple warm days to heat everything up a couple degrees will push the catfish to feed more aggressively.

Late Summer/Early Fall
Water Temperature Falling

Water temperature falling is just part of this time of year. It is normal to see the hot water of summer come down as the days get shorter and the nights get cooler.

Normally, you will see a slight drop in temperature over time and it really does not affect much in the catfish bite.

Sometimes, you will run into a stiff cold front that will drop the water temperature a lot, sometimes six to ten degrees in just a couple days. When this happens, the fish will feel it and get sluggish in a hurry. They can experience a 50 or more percent decrease in metabolism.

Now it is a time to get out of the current in rivers. The fish will be off current (usually in the shallows) or deep in cover or structure to sulk.

The way to catch these fish is to get bait in the areas they are lying and be prepared to sit on them longer. Sometimes it takes 30-40 minutes to get one of these sluggish fish to take the bait compared to the normal 15-20 minutes.

Late Summer/Early Fall
Water Level Rising

During summer and fall, if the water rises a small amount, not much will change in terms of where you will find them. Should the river see a dramatic increase in flow, the catfish tend to migrate to the secondary seam along the banks and hold tight in snags. In case of flooding, they may make larger moves to less hostile conditions.

Late Summer/Early Fall
Water Level Stable to Falling

Water levels stable to falling is a normal summer phenomenon. It is very normal to experience stable water levels with very slow declines in flow and levels. When conditions are normal, fish as you would in a normal to rising water temperature.

In the case of dramatic falling water levels after a flood or big rain, fish off the main channel in the secondary seams and near current. The catfish tend not to feed in fast dropping water. They get off current and sit tight waiting for conditions to improve. Fish slowly and off the current, sitting on spots 20-50 percent longer to allow the catfish time to find the bait and commit to it.

OBSERVATION: Pay attention to the banks during this time of year. This time of year tends to be lower water levels. By paying attention to the banks you will know where fishable structure is when water levels are high in the future.

Late Summer/Early Fall
Barometer High or Rising

This is a time when the barometer is the most important.
When the barometer is rising, it usually means a storm
recently passed or there is a weather system of clear, hot
weather. This is a time when the fish will look for shade
or deeper water during the day. They may also move to a
morning/evening or all-out night bite. When fishing
during the day, fish deeper holes with current nearby. You
will have to cover a lot of water to find active fish.

Late Summer/Early Fall
Barometer Falling

A falling barometer can mean a small cold front moving through that has little or no effect on the catfish, or it can be an indicator to an all out storm. If the weather man tells you there is a chance of severe weather over the next 24-48 hours, get ready because the catfish are in preparation mode. Fish aggressively covering a lot of water, looking for strong feeding areas such as heads of holes, troughs and outside bends.

In lakes, especially lakes with underwater channels or creeks, the catfish will be feeding on the edges.

A slow falling barometer can indicate a good bite, as a lower or falling barometer means cloudy, and catfish tend to be more active in low light or night. The simple fact that clouds can cut heat could turn a bite on.

Late Summer/Early Fall
Light Conditions

Sunny

When the water temperature is on the higher end of the spectrum during this part of the season, you may have to fish the sunny times like you would during the summer. As we get into the cooler nights and the water temps begin to fall, sunny days begin to have less bearing on the catfish.

Cloudy

During the late summer and fall, partly cloudy days can be fantastic. It is a transition time, so some clouds and sun can push the fish to feed. Again, the barometer is typically dropping on cloudy days and this sometimes is a trigger for catfish to feed.

Dark

Fishing at night during the late summer/early fall times can be some of the most productive fishing you can encounter. At the beginning of this time it can still be hot outside, pushing the fish to feed at night. As the water temps begin to cool, the feeding heats up and the fish will feed aggressively and can be very shallow.

Late Summer/Early Fall
Water Clarity

Water Clear
If the water is clear, the sun will have more effect on the day bite in hot conditions. Think deeper or in cover when the sun is high and hot.

Water Cloudy or Dirty
Dirty water blocks sun penetration that may bother the catfish. With silt in the water and less sun penetration, cats will be more willing to sit in shallower water and feed during the day.

FALL

Fall can be mixed in with part of the process used in the Late Summer/Early Fall because the times cross over and the patterns begin to change from day to day.

We all know that fall is when the catfish put on the feed bags in preparation for the cold water that is ahead. Some of the information is the same as we move from Early Fall and into Fall Cold Water.

This is a time when lateral movement comes into play more than any other time. Catfish metabolism is falling and depending on whether the water is warming or cooling will determine the mood of the day and where the catfish are. When they are feeding, they will be in the current or the edges of holes or break lines in lakes.

When the catfish are negative, they will get out of the current and sit. This may be very shallow in a river or in a deep hole in a lake.

Fall
Water Temperature 70-60 Degrees and Falling

This time of year, the water temperature is beginning to fall and that is normal. When it normally falls off just a few degrees per week, the catfish will actually kick into high gear and feed hard. In this situation, fish just like you did in summer, with the exception of looking shallow (even during the day) as instinct will have them in full hunting mode.

Should a huge cold front come through and drop the water temperature more than five degrees in a couple days, you should change gears and get out of the current. The fish have not moved far but are more sluggish and will be out of the current, usually shallow right along bank. Sit on them a little longer than you normally would to allow them time to find the bait and decide to take it.

Refer to drawing on page 105

Fall
Water Temperature 70-60 Degrees and Rising

During this time the catfish should be feeding well anyway, but a little warm up can really kick them into high gear. Just the opposite of when the water temperature is falling, be prepared to fish aggressively. Move out to the main current seams and be willing to fish faster.

Refer to drawing on page 103

Fall
Water Temperature 60-50 Degrees and Falling

This is a critical period in the seasonal progression of catfish. They know the end is near. Their metabolism has fallen by nearly 70 percent in fairly short order, yet they know they have to feed to prepare for the big move to the wintering holes where they will potentially not be feeding much over the next few months.

It is normal to fish the off currents of rivers and be prepared to sit on spots a little longer. Keep working structure and shallow, out of the current areas and you will find active catfish mixed in.

Refer to drawing on page 104

Fall
Water Temperature 60-50 Degrees and Rising

Even a degree increase in water temperature can make a good catfishing day a great catfishing day; the clock is ticking and any increase in water temperature is a big deal. It doesn't take cats much to notice the change and get into the feeding areas.

Fall
Water Level Rising

Normally in fall, rising water is not a thing we have to contend with. But if it does happen, especially during the early part of the fall pattern, it can be amazing. The catfish feed upstream in rivers and a rise in the water can make them feed almost as if it were a pre spawn bite.

If the water were to come up fast as the fish are beginning to make their annual downstream migration to the wintering holes, they may be forced up tributaries or farther downstream than they go in a normal year.

Refer to drawing on page 104

Fall
Water Level Stable to Falling

A stable to slow decrease in water level is a very normal part of fall. Not much changes as far as the bite goes if this is happening.

In the case of a fast drop from a high water period, the fish will be pushed out of the main channel and into the secondary channel just like during the spawn period. As soon as it settles out, the fish will move to the wintering areas.

Refer to drawing on page 102

Fall

Barometer Rising

A rising barometer won't have much bearing on catfish at this time. It will tend to push them to the deeper part of the holes, but it should come with a warming trend. The small increase in water temperature it creates could spur some feeding. If the fish are not biting in the holes, move out to the edges to see if this is what is happening.

Barometer Falling

As with any other season, a falling barometer tends to lend itself to lower light and a negative force coming in. This will spur some feeding. In this case, be at the edges or front of the holes to attract any feeding fish that may be out preparing.

Fall
Light Conditions

Sunny

Light can play a very key role in fall catfishing. Metabolism is on the way down, equivalent to pre spawn when it is on the way up. A sunny day or two can warm the water a bit more and get the fish feeding a little more aggressively, as the cold water period looms.

Sun will warm the shallows first then the deeper water along the break lines. On sunny days start shallow first before moving deeper as the day goes on and feeding gets more aggressive.

Cloudy

If conditions are cloudy start shallow and expect the fish to be shallow or right on the break line of holes. Again, a cloudy day can indicate a front and falling barometer triggering feeding.

Dark

Like any other time of the year catfish will feed at night.

FALL COLD WATER

Fall Cold Water

The fall cold water period is pretty much the spring cold water period in reverse. Instead of the metabolism picking up with each degree of water temperature and the fish becoming more active, the metabolism and activity decreases with every degree of decrease in water temperature.

As the water temperature cools, the fish will settle into the wintering holes and areas for the long winter ahead. They will not quit feeding, but they do not require much food during this time to survive.

The key to successful catching is to find numbers of fish and play the averages that somebody has to eat.

Fall Cold Water
Water Temperature 50-40 Degrees

This is the point when most catfish anglers hang up the rods. The catfish begin to make their move to the wintering holes and set up for the long winter ahead.

In rivers, there are still some catfish feeding and they can be caught using normal techniques, but it seems that they are mostly hanging out of the current and are very finicky.

This is a time to downsize your gear and your bait. Be on guard to feel the bites and set the hooks, because the fish can bite very lightly.

In ponds and lakes, the catfish move to the same deeper areas and congregate for the winter. They will still bite, but you have to work the edges of the holes and be patient to find the active fish in the area.

This is the time the blue catfishing starts to really pick up for the season. Downsizing gear may not be a good idea if you are fishing in blue catfish waters.

Fall Cold Water
Water Temperature 40-32 Degrees

The fish have settled into the holes for the long winter ahead. This is a great time to start jigging catfish. How big of catfish you have will depend on how stout of gear you will need.

Because the catfish are so sluggish, you can get away with a medium to medium heavy jigging rod to feel the lightest of bites. Don't worry, because the fish won't make the big runs like they do during the warmer times of year.

Working the outer edges of holes to find the active fish is key. Fish slowly and let the fish find the bait.

If you are fishing a lake or reservoir with a channel, work the outer edges of the channel and the holes.

This time fishing catfish is similar to fishing ice cats. Right before freeze up, you can fish these same wintering holes using many of the same techniques

Refer to drawing on pages 102, 110

Fall Cold Water
Water Rising

Should there be a significant event of precipitation causing a rise in water, it may push the fish to relocate to the off current areas. Just like spring cold water during the flood seasons, the fish will move to more hospitable areas.

They may move up into creeks and other tributaries until conditions settle back down.

Water Level Stable to Falling

Stable to slow dropping water is common in the fall, which would make conditions normal based on what was stated in the patterns for the cold water patterns.

Keep working the outer edges of the holes or the channels to find the active fish that are feeding.

Fall Cold Water
Barometer Rising

Like any other time of the season, a rising barometer may put conditions in place to allow for catfish to sit a little tighter and eat only when they absolutely have to.

Barometer Falling

The barometer still dictates what is about to happen and it is instinctual for catfish to feed as an impending negative may be moving in. The drop in barometer leading up to a storm or weather system can trigger feeding.

This may be a good time to target drop off areas of holes or even the front of holes or the flats ahead of holes.

In lakes, fish the outer edges of holes and flats near holes.

Fall Cold Water
Light Conditions

The days are getting shorter and there is just not much warmth getting into the water during this time. With very little need to feed, if all other conditions are stable, the old "fish at low light" times comes into play.

The best times to fish are a couple of hours before sunrise and at first light, as well as the last hour until sunset and into the first hours of darkness.

ICE CATS

Ice fishing for catfish is limited to the northern region. In some areas it is fairly tough, while in others fairly simple. The one key is putting in the time to locate the areas where the catfish have holed up for winter. From that point, it is just a matter of playing the conditions like any other time of the year.

There are a few things to consider with catfish under the ice versus catfish during other times of the year. Being a warm water fish, catfish don't require much food to survive during this period, which causes feeding to be sporadic. It also makes them very sluggish and they will not attack baits like they do during the warm times of the year. Keep your jigging motion to a minimum or even almost no jigging at all.

Ice Cats
Normal Feeding Conditions

Catfish under ice don't feed much so once you locate the areas that are holding the fish, it is time to find a shelf or structure near the hole along the edge. This will be the ambush point for hunting catfish.

The best locations in rivers or reservoirs is to find large deep holes that can hold many catfish. Due to them not needing to feed much, the fact that they have the numbers in these locations means that somebody has to feed. This is simply using the numbers to your advantage to find active catfish.

Ice Cats
Barometer Rising

As the barometer rises after a front or on a sunny day, it is important to consider that there may not be much movement along the edges. Besides working the normal spots, consider fishing closer to the school, or even in the school, in case someone decides they want you are offering.

Barometer falling

Like any other time of the year, an approaching storm front may spur a feeding situation in preparation of the negative effects of the storm. This a great time to get on the edges of channels and on the transition lines, to head off any catfish that move up and hunt.

Ice Cats
Time of Day

Time of day is probably more important to ice cats than it is during any other time of the season. As mentioned before, the metabolism of a catfish under the ice is very low, meaning they only need to feed at the optimum times.

In most cases, the catfish bite is best an hour before sunset and into darkness or very early in the morning before the sun rises and for about an hour after.

Refer to drawing on page 110

ELECTRONICS

One element that was never really brought up in this book is electronics. There is a reason for the absence and it is simple. Not everyone has high-end electronics or in some cases, electronics at all. This system of catching catfish has been brought back to the most basic of levels, to help you better understand the catfish and the waters that they call home.

Let's take a moment to discuss how one might use electronics matched with the understanding of the conditions of this book.

Electronics are changing the catfishing world for everyone from the shore to the boat. Of course the electronics can go as far as your imagination and pocketbook want to take you.

If you fish from shore, there are many new high quality electronics that can have a transducer hooked to a line and cast out. As it is reading the bottom, it will wirelessly send back the depths and other information to a smart phone or other wireless device. These systems, with a little time and creativity, can allow a shore angler to get a good understanding of holes, break lines and even to see fish.

Of course the boat people get the advantage of being mobile to find fish and utilize advanced electronics. Most catfish anglers have at least a depth finder. Many are now moving into side imaging or at least down imaging, as prices come down.

Side imaging is very useful with catfishing, especially in the systems of this book. It allows an angler to drive past a spot that should hold fish and see what structure may be under the water, how the fish are relating to it or if there are even fish in the area.

New and quickly gaining ground, is live map-making software in sonar units. this allows an angler to map the once uncharted catfish waters to mark and save depth structures. It can be paired with side imaging to make a map and see all of the structure located in an area.

It used to take a whole summer to figure out the lay of a hole and the structure within. Now it takes about ten minutes.

Technology will continue to advance and become more affordable as time goes on.

If you use the systems of this book to better understand where the fish should be. You can then implement your electronics to prove the fish are there. From there you will be able to build upon the information provided and be more successful.

CONCLUSION

Catfishing is a very popular, growing and ever-changing sport. At this time, the surface is just being scratched as to how far it will go. It is my hope that you find this book useful in your catfishing endeavors for years to come. I want this to help you be consistent in landing more and bigger catfish.

Just remember nature plays by nature's rules. We are fishing not catching and the best teacher is time on the water. Hard work matched with a solid knowledge of the fish WILL make you successful!

GLOSSARY

Current- The flow of water influenced by gravity as the water moves downhill to reduce its potential energy.

Current Seam- The line formed in current where faster water and slower water meet. Usually by a dropoff in a river channel.

Lateral Movement- For the purpose of fishing rivers, let's first define and explain lateral movement and how it works.

Lateral movement is a simple pattern that says catfish in rivers do not run up and down a river based on conditions. It means that when catfish are active, they will move laterally across a river channel to more aggressive feeding spots and when the conditions make them more sluggish, they will move away from the heavy current of the feeding spots to rest and recuperate.

This does not mean they are not feeding at all, it just means that they adjust where they will holed up (on current or off current) depending on the conditions.

Metabolism- Chemical process that occurs to break down food and sustain life.

Off Current- The area that is just out of the main current of a stream or river. Sometimes referred to as secondary current.

Structure- Geology or other items such as trees that create a current break or drop off for a fish to relate to.

Tributary- A smaller stream or river that runs into a larger stream or river.

RIVER DIAGRAMS
Graphics designed by Ann White

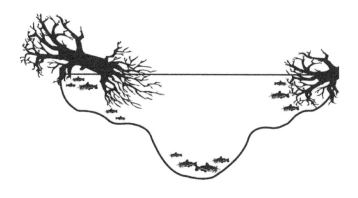

This is a cross section of how a basic river would look. It shows how the fish will move laterally into the main channel to feed aggressively, as well as how they might use structure to get out of the current during certain times.

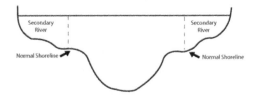

This cross section of a river shows the river when full. It demonstrates how the normal level shoreline creates the secondary current channels and quite literally a river of its own.

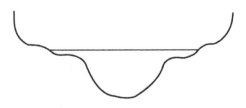

This cross section of a river shows the river is at normal pool. It shows how a river would look if you cut a chunk out and looked at it the long way. This shows you where the current seams might set up along the channels.

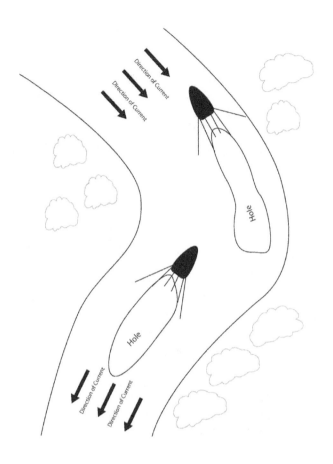

This drawing shows a river in normal conditions. It shows basic setup on holes. These holes can be located on the outside bends and in the middle of the river. The fish usually relate to the current and the feeding conditions.

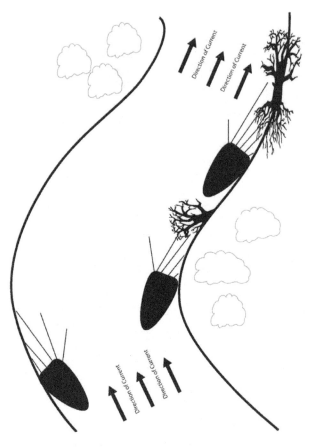

Here you see a river in normal pool. During spring or spawn season, you might fish the inside bends depicted by the sandbars just off the current. In normal feeding conditions, you would likely find fish on the edge of the channel at the outside bend.

The dots along the bank notate where spawning holes in the bank may be located.

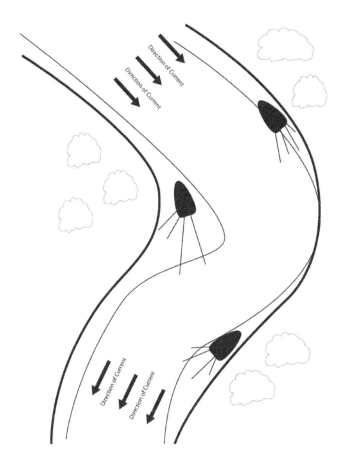

This drawing depicts a high river and demonstrates how you might fish along the secondary current lines. Notice it is right up against the bank in most cases and on the back of an inside corner or an area where the channel has turned away from the bank.

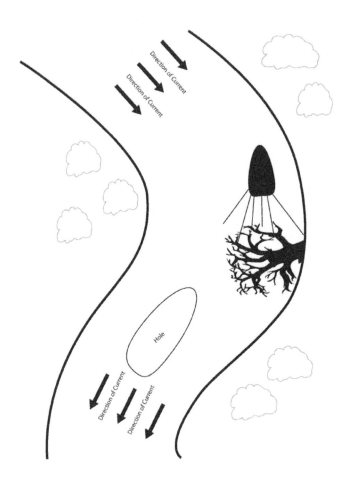

This drawing shows more normal conditions with a mid-river hole that may hold fish. It also has a snag on the outside bend where the current may have dug out a channel. This is a good location to find resting fish waiting to ambush an easy meal.

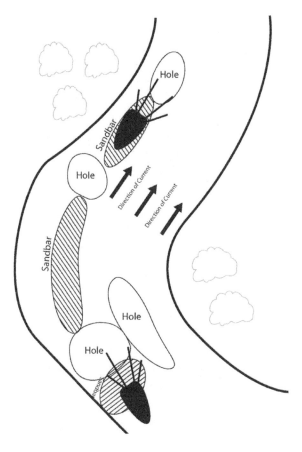

Here we have a situation where sandbars have formed in a stretch of river. These hard sandbars usually have holes carved out behind them, forming holes for easy resting and feeding for catfish. Some of these holes may be very small but hold very big fish. Simply anchor on top of or next to the sandbar and cast into the hole. If you are on shore, you can simply cast to the hole.

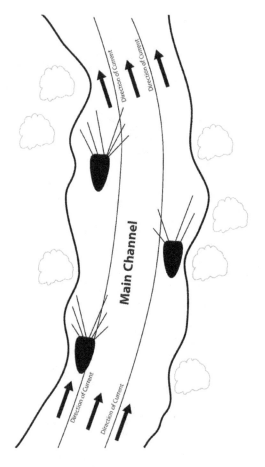

This drawing depicts a new pattern of feeding times during the spring and fall. This is the area where the catfish will lay in very shallow water in these little nooks along the bank. To locate fish, simply cast into the nook and fish for 15-20 minutes. If no fish, move to the next one. One of the best ways to find fish in these spots is use side image sonar to tell you if they are in the nook.

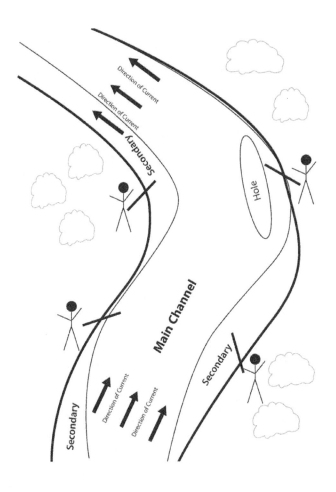

This is a very rough drawing of how some of this might look from a shore perspective. (It is understood that nobody looks like a stick.) If the water is rising, high or during a spawn, you will want to look for spots that look similar to the one marked "secondary current". If conditions are normal, you will want to look at the outside edges or near structure (not shown) or holes.

This can be modified to any one of the other drawings in this book.

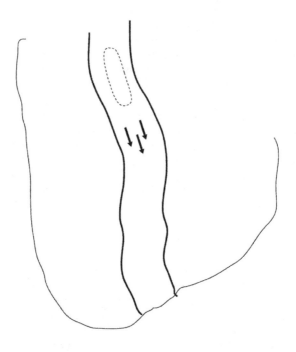

This drawing shows an old channel within a lake or reservoir. This old channel is the key to finding feeding catfish. They will use it for feeding and traveling around in the lake. Deeper spots will hold fish during hot weather and during the cold water times. During feeding times, the catfish will move away from the deeper water to the break lines.

ABOUT CAPTAIN BRAD DURICK

Captain Brad Durick is a nationally known professional catfish guide, writer, educator and speaker based on the Red River of the North at Grand Forks, North Dakota.

Durick has appeared in numerous articles and television shows teaching the finer points of catching catfish. He is the author of the 2013 book *Cracking the Channel Catfish Code*. His first book contains groundbreaking research on channel catfish and river conditions, as well as the original pattern called "lateral movement", which is perhaps the single biggest catfishing breakthrough in decades.

Captain Brad is available for a guided catfish trip of a lifetime or to speak at your next show or event. Contact him at 701-739-5808 or www.redrivercatfish.com

Made in United States
Orlando, FL
03 May 2023

32748365R00065